London Bridge

SIMON SMITH is the author of three books of poetry, *Fifteen Exits* (2001), *Reverdy Road* (2003) and *Mercury* (2006). Two pamphlets of poetry have appeared since — *Telegraph Cottage* co-authored with Felicity Allen (2007), and *Browning Variations* (2009). He also translates Latin and French poetry, and has written for *Poetry Review* and *PN Review*. He worked at the Poetry Library from 1991–2007, and in 2004 he was a judge of the National Poetry Prize. He is a lecturer in creative writing at the University of Kent, and was a Hawthornden Fellow (2009).

Also by Simon Smith

BOOKS
Fifteen Exits (Waterloo Press)
Reverdy Road (Salt)
Mercury (Salt)

PAMPHLETS
North Star (Poetical Histories)
LEXICON (Form Books)
Night Shift (Prest Roots)
Juicy Fruit (Gratton Street Irregulars)
Telegraph Cottage [with Felicity Allen] (Seeing Eye)
Browning Variations (Landfill)

WORKS OF TRANSLATION
Notice to Quit by Gaius Valerius Catullus (Verisimilitude)
My Heart Is In My Pocket: Poems by Pierre Reverdy (Verisimilitude)

London Bridge

SIMON SMITH

SALT

LONDON

PUBLISHED BY SALT PUBLISHING
Fourth Floor, 2 Tavistock Place, Bloomsbury, London WC1H 9RA United Kingdom

Salt Publishing 2010

Printed and bound in the United Kingdom by Lightning Source UK Ltd

Typeset in Swift 9.5 / 13

ISBN 978 1 84471 490 2 paperback

1 3 5 7 9 8 6 4 2

for Flick, again, and also for David Rees

'all you had to know was the answers' — ORNETTE COLEMAN

Contents

Acknowledgements

Some of these poems appeared in the following publications, sometimes in different versions:

fragmente: a magazine of contemporary poetics number 9 2007 for 'Orpheus. Eurydice. Hermes (after Rilke)'. *Lamport Court* number 8 2007 for 'Deep Breath', 'Least Most', 'Oyster Card'. *Limelight* Issue 15: March 2008 for 'Objects of Desire', 'A Table', 'How They Brought the Good News from Ghent to Aix', 'A 53 or a 172' and 'About the Mountain'. Manchester Poetry Festival 2005 for 'Imagist Poem'. *Painted, spoken* number 8 2005 for 'Stereogram'. *Painted, spoken* number 13 2008 for 'Designs' and 'First Idea'. *Poems for Remembrance Day*, Sky Arts 2006 for 'The Auburn Stunner (after Apollinaire)'. *PN Review* 171, Volume 33 Number 1 September–October 2006 for 'Martial, I.7', 'V.20', 'V.34', 'V.37', 'X.47', 'X.61'.

My thanks to these editors, producers and photographers: Huw Briggs, Dean Farrow, Chris McCabe, Anthony Mellors, Richard Price, David Rees, Michael Schmidt, and Matthew Welton.

Also thank you to Dr Martin Gaskill and everyone at Hawthornden Castle for providing me with a Hawthornden Fellowship in the summer of 2009 to finalise the text of this book. I also offer grateful thanks to the other Fellows at Hawthornden for their camaraderie: Khalid Alkanissi, Mary Finn, Cliff Forshaw, Kathryn Maris and G.C. Waldrep.

And many thanks to Flick, Stanley and Dorothy for all their support whilst writing this collection.

On Telegraph Hill

I.

Dornier, Heinkel, Junkers, and ME 110 queue from Calais
To north-west Kent, fast shapes sweep time
Delayed piston, thunder, whine over
Suburban Surrey, down Sussex Downs. St. Paul's their hub

Circling, the swarm begun to storm, big black splashes
Darken paving stones, soon a downpour. Black cloud
Of Ruskin's nightmare, Denmark Hill to Brantwood.
Drrrrum rumrumrum drrrum rumrumrum drrrum rumrumrum

II.

Click. The washing-machine ends its cycle.
Families sit late, sunlit on stripy deck chairs,
Heads swiveled up, eyes swimming to the late,
Late summer showers, rows of shiny business class

Criss-cross sight-lines with flight paths in secret
Cross-hairs, feel their way down the spokes and invisible
Corridors of power to Heathrow, landing safe as houses.
Out of the airport lobby, the mad dash to the next working lunch.

Address

I moved in today.

Could be good, judging by the weather

And the lack of traffic getting here,

But probably not a good idea, on reflection

I thought not a time for recording

Thoughts, what with boxes packed, airless

Carrier bags, mica shelving, brackets,

The stereo and all those stairs.

Dogs nosing about below the bedroom window

Calls across the street,

Mothers to toddlers

Oven chips, ketchup, bed.

That order.

Martial, Book I Poem 7

My friend Stella's favourite is Maximus,
His dove (dare I say it and Verona hears!)
Passes Catullus' sparrow beyond measure.
My friend Stella eye-balls your Catullus,
Just like a dove weighs in against a sparrow.

CCTV

Sit in the front seat
Miss the mesh. Ditto mess
Michelle there
And not there
Data tingles the light
Bulb peeling white
Indoor undercoat
Applied to outdoor woodwork
The whole planet jumped 2cm to the left
Smooth blinds drawn
To moonlight slatted one-way street
Cut into horizontal strips
Scientific mythology of the once
Perfectly reasonable
A car approaches then recedes
Drenching a wall of data
Crashing through a fine spray
The point as good as a CD
Wiped emulsion
Great buckets of Reality

Ode on a Grecian Urn

I'm wearing odd socks nobody can tell, but I know.
When a glider tug struggles against the jet-stream to the high blue yonder
Its message clearly 'JUNGLE NIGHTS AT EDEN MON–THURS'
Bold and glowing in Arial, the drone then recedes.
Mr Genius is comfortable enough leaning forwards against Infinity,
Or God only knows what, bursting through his Mr Genius tee-shirt.
The juggling Mr Ezra Pound cycles
The tow-path on his trike mistaken for Niké,
And Michelle's eyes more distant than the distant stars,
The light notation of once present shadows
Now a single thin and slight radio wave. Isn't Nature wonderful!
She being a phone-call away and sweet as a drop down menu!
She leans back on the verandah, sipping the sparkle from her mineral
    water
To kick off her flat shoes, as speed boats skip past like flat stones,
The synchronicity of it:
So Chance and Procedure are file-sharing with Truth and Beauty,
'To see how things go' is one incredible finishing line, and all you need to
    know.

Bob's Day

Pulls into shape
A wireless connection
Talks to bits
Chromium hinge
Holm oaks to the native
Japanese anemone
Cistus poppy
Dog-rose
Licked with urban
Insect activity
Ancient species
Rainwater butts
Full to burst
Boughs flutter
A parliament

Online O.E.D.

Get on the bus
Get off the bus
The cake is made of diamonds
Throw in the Jack the Knave
Of diamonds, the cake is made of chemicals
Held in particular
Vapour falling away
Comfy jumbo hotdogs
The fragrance of lilies
A throw away fuzzy fellow
Tries to keep the place tidy
Something sharpens its beak
On the branches of a dead tree

That Love Thing
(after Propertius, Elegies, II.15)

I'm in heaven after a glittering night! And you,
    prized of mattresses, covered with my pleasure,
How much chatter with burning the midnight oil,
    how many thrashings around after 'lights out'!
At first she'd battle frantically, bare-chested,
    then she would draw up her nightie, teasing.
As I dropped asleep she brushed my eyes with her lips
    and the words, 'wake up, wake up, layabout.'
How multiple the forms of our lovemaking,
    how we frenched for the entire duration!
It's purposeless corrupting Love as sights unseen:
    you need to know—love's in the forward glance.
Paris was consumed gazing upon Helen nude
    as she arose from Menelaus' bed;
The nude Endymion entranced Phoebus' sister,
    and, so they say, nude he laid the goddess.
Insist if you must, sleeping in night-clothes, I swear
    I'll shred your night-dress with feverish hands
And should my frantic ire inspire me all the more—
    your arms black and blue to show your mother.
You've no cause for shame with heavy breasts made to love;
    that's for her too uptight to bear children.
Let us take the chance and gorge our eyes on good looks:
    one everlasting night, day never dawns.
If only we were tied each to each as we hug,
    that not for one day may we pass apart.
Let us take the loving doves, paired for our example,
    male and female conjugally perfect.
He makes a mistake creating rules for passion;
    truth is: real love knows not when to stop.
The earth proves false to peasants sowing the wrong seed,
    the Sun might thrash black horses through heaven,
And the waterways suck back their flow to the head,
    drawing oceans dry to leave fish gasping
Before I substitute this love for another.

I belong to her in death as in life.
If she could concede a night here or there like this,
    a year represents a life's achievements;
Offer a multitude, my place immortalised.
    Just one night's stay raises man to god.
If every man wanted to live their life like mine,
    at leisure, arms and legs droopy with wine
There would be no vicious blades or war galleons,
    Actium's waves would not break on our bones,
Nor Rome, often victim of her own ambitions,
    shy away from proper displays of grief.
This thing our forebears will grace with certitude:
    our skirmishes never caused gods fury.
But dear, if the sun's out desert not life's chances,
    shower me with kisses—they're not enough!
As flower petals fall, shedding from dying wreaths
    blown all over to bob in wine glasses,
So we who desire with all our senses heightened
    might find our new days fated as our last.

A 53 or a 172

Breathe in the shape of an ice cube,
As the inspector flashes a white-gold ring.

Dad wears a black singlet. One stop,
Then home. Silver Nikes for the kids.
Some sit, some prefer to stand, some shout:
Indices flapping arms up and down
The Old Kent Road where the 'action'
Is, performance in international and local

Markets, split dividends, so the question
Stands like a beggar, and the rude girls go:

'Do do-do do-do do do-do do do-do do-do
Do do-do do do-do do-do do do-do do do-do

Do-do do do-do do do-do do-do do do-do do
Do-do do-do do do-doooooooooooooooooooooo'

'Chaucer, he can make you say any think
That Chaucer can talk it up chatting shit.'

Personal Note

Let's meet, discuss plumbing, give up phone conferences, be happy.
Pink cloud tinged, a little sunlight to offices, London clays all walks
Of human life. I take the opposite view, but no matter. Peeling white
Paint, yellow brick houses opposite of unconnected events and concepts,
A series for no reason but the London hum: brick property, bottle the
    person
Not a philosophy maybe, but as metropolitan logic runs deep, easy to
    follow.

Michael

My bank account has a mind of its own
Let's call it Michael after Michael
Stipe — Michelle's brother-for-a-day —
It breathes, speaks, makes phone calls
Using my mobile! A place to say what
You don't believe, which is suddenly
Interesting, grazing idea by idea.
Stick-men hobble over snow outside,
Inaudible footsteps, large flake after
Large flake, like snow-shoes grey glow,
Thin morning sunshine across wet grass
Where are they going in their quest
Their need to know the answers?
But Michael keeps me occupied — the financial
Inducements cause one to roll over:
This is, in truth, utter solitude. Furthermore,
What is in Paul's interesting bag:
One question which insists
In the asking.

Anniversaries

So, we tripped over
Ourselves and doorsteps
Not a valentine
And over toys small
Hours run quickly by
Too many to count
I gave up at seven
A pretty flower
Like a bad smell
Brilliant orange
Katherine Hepburn said
In *The African*
Queen: those marigolds
Feed them the bottle
Of flat fizzy water.

So, we tripped over
Not a valentine
Hours run quickly by
I gave up at seven
Like a bad smell
Katherine Hepburn said
Queen: those marigolds
Of flat fizzy water
Feed them the bottle
In *The African*
Brilliant orange
A pretty flower
Too many to count
And over toys small
Ourselves and doorsteps

So, we tripped over
Hours run quickly by
Like a bad smell
Queen: those marigolds
Feed them the bottle
Brilliant orange
Too many to count
Ourselves and doorsteps
And over toys small
A pretty flower
In The African
Of flat fizzy water
Katherine Hepburn said
I gave up at seven
Not a valentine

So, we tripped over
Like a bad smell
Feed them the bottle
Too many to count
And over toys small
In *The African*
Katherine Hepburn said
Not a valentine
I gave up at seven
Of flat fizzy water
A pretty flower
Ourselves and doorsteps
Brilliant orange
Queen: those marigolds
Hours run quickly by

'Bye, bye'

Nude descending a stair. Look, another version of it strides by
To reinforce that sense of a journey, a purpose, albeit stutteringly

≈

(Drum roll)

≈

Buy it out of the box

≈

That's my philosophy, 'don't look back,'
The late afternoon light failing

≈

The crate of beer rattles down the yard, the years,
And the office workers, where do they go?

≈

Which brings me bang up-to-date and the echoed click of the keyboard,
The reminder, the mnemonics. It comes out this way

≈

And now to split the atom. Any atom.

≈

Picture the scene tap-dancing over cold-cuts

The re-arranging of deck-chairs. My back garden under
International Arrivals

~

From the toilet the perfect smell of pink
Chemicals fused with cleanesses' moral imperative

~

Drizzle. The ice I imagine.

~

A few short things.

~

For my next trick the fusion of ideas with ideals.

~

On this occasion—occasional.

~

A few more. Short things.

~

250 more grams of Lurpak. 'You are what you eat.'
No longer the myth of youth, or yesterday

∾

Or think out of it

∾

More importantly, 'where have they been?' Ian Curtis
enquires.

Green Shield Stamps

(Subtitled: lines between parentheses

Or italics for emphasis).

Kinda like Baudelaire *without* the knobs on.

Shots side-by-side, the pint of Guinness,

Neatly *sur la table*, 'bespoke' so to speak (spoken for).

Read and reflect on the wrong-doings of the day

Flexing my Juan-Gris-attention-span,

My life transparent through broadsheets.

'After counselling, 'issues,' trauma . . .' etc.

But *still* no answer, laughter

And tears signal the 'all clear.'

Take the instruction.

And you can sign off 'yourself.'

Stereogram

Light filed to narrow sharpness
Skates close
Mistaken you
Feel the brush of breath
Against your neck like new,
And how apt I witness partly
A female blackbird her sing-song
Clear, a freshness
Tawny out on the London air
Partly above, higher
Was that the bit swung up sharply
To repeat, adept, surely as needle
Trips vinyl, genuine reproductions
Cars, bikes, buses, taxis, trucks
Emergency services' flaming sirens
Part mix, part shout, part part,
Part dub, part bass, part horn,
Part chorus, part whisper,
Part honk, part loop, part
Solo, part squeal, part
Found, part lost

Orpheus. Eurydice. Hermes.
(after Rilke)

This bottomless pit of shadows.
Like silvery trails, they soundlessly
Skated on into the endless void. Lifeblood drowned
Low-lying vegetation, following its route to the earth's surface,
Where dusk fell, it solidified as feldspar.
Nothing redder in sight.

A precipice soared skyward,
And forests thick as fog. Swaying footbridges
Reached into the blackness, and a huge, grey, sightless lake
Mirrored the heights to the bottomless drop
Of a sky over hills and valleys, filtered through gloomy daylight.
Across tranquil fields
A public bridleway unravelled like calico.

Down this road they came.

Leading, a thin man draped in blue—
silent, an angsty, shifty gaze, arrow-like, forward.
With long, fast strides he quick-marched,
Eating up the distance; hands straight down
Making tight fists, punching out the greatcoat's creases,
Unaware of the priceless lyre
That grew from his left side, like a bunch
Of lifeless roses taped around an olive branch.
His senses hewn in two parts;
His power of seeing far ahead like a sheepdog
Corrals and swerves,
Upright, to attention, quivering at the furthest corner—
His listening like a smell motionless in the air it floats in.
Occasionally, he caught it, hung about
As far back as the footfall of the others
Who ought to shadow him up the footpath to sunshine.
No, it was no more than his own echoing back,
No more than the breeze rustling his coat.

They're still with me, he told himself;
Whispered out loud to die on the air.
They were there, he had to believe, grave doubts rushed
In to fill their lightness of foot. Desperate to cast his hungry gaze
Behind, knowing the look would obliterate
The entire expedition, so nearly
Realised, and if he did, if he did he could not help but see
The two, cautious, ghosting him distantly:

He, god of quickness, long-distance and Director of
     Communications,
The brim of his cap pulled tight over beady eyes,
His walking-stick thrust before him,
At his ankles tiny wings beating the silence;
At his side, upheld on his left hand, as pledged: she.

She, adored at such a pitch, one lone lyre sang
A full-throated sadness more sustained than
The entire profession of mourners since the earth was born,
The drone re-creating the earth, in its slopes
And copses and tracks and settlements
And meadows and rivers and beasts;
With its own sun orbiting this other world of sadness
Parallel to this normal world, a second sun floated,
Through this veil of tears pregnant with heavenly bodies.
She, adored at this pitch.

From here she stepped to the left of the god,
Her little feet tightened by the winding-sheet,
Unsure, timid, unafraid.
Deep in her own thoughts, as a woman expecting,
And recognised neither the other ahead,
Nor the track rising to the places alive above.

Deep in her own thoughts. Her deathly state
Shrouded her, her great prize beyond want.
Like fruit sugared in its own decay,
She was satiated with the enormity of death,
The shock of its newness beyond her comprehension.

She had entered her new maidenhood
Where no one could touch her; her petals were shut
Tight as a nightshade, her wedding finger
Sore with the constrictions of wedlock
So the god's infinitely subtle attentions
Scalded her, like cold lips unsought for.

No longer the bombshell
Whose Being dictated poem after poem back to him;
She was his lost love-seat's perfume, and his rock:
A step away from him.

She was shaken free as long hair,
Random and scattered as a rain shower,
Sown far and wide as grain.

Rooted to the spot. She.

At that moment the god pulled up sharp.
Stopped her in her tracks and said,
Voice quivering: he looks behind!
Confused, eyes opened wide, she whispered: who?

Miles away, a shadow in the glowing exit,
Somebody, A.N. Other in silhouette,
Nose, eyes, mouth, unremarkable.
He was there, compelled to watch
The God of Communications turning back
On the path between the fields, weeping

Soundless, tuck in behind the slight body
Turned shuffling along the track,
Feet tightened by the winding-sheet,
Unsure, timid, unafraid.

'A' for Apple

Laid on by Eve, the temptation of Snow White, Aphrodite's prize,
Branded tart, a Bramley, a soft Cox or greenest Golden Delicious?

In the 'On' Position

One minute life's like that.
The Cambridge Book of Slang.
Flintstone faces under duvets like puffy clouds.
Michelle's best mate shall remain nameless.
But she's a Tory.
The pink gloves' hot inner life clean the Command Center,
Lend the impermanence of a human touch.
Rainstorm clouds stream past tinted windows.
Purple succulents in the way
Knowledge is information
Half writing half the thing half not thinking
Flips function for function

Imagist Poem

Vauxhall Cresta before I die
I will drive one. Authentic
Red leather bench seat, smell of calf
And pipe smoke. Automatic.
Two-tone bottle-green
And peppermint, aromatic
Big red tail lights. Fins.

Operating System

Gregor Samsa rattles across my poorly lit desk. I translate the
timbre of questions answered by silence, somewhere between
plaster, mortar and brick, a reasoned argument, obviously lodged.
The neighbours grumble through the lower registers.

Twenty-five blooming narcissi, enough for a classroom, blink
opposite. Half-empty thoughts half-full, tubes, fibres, strands
coincidental as cauliflower ear, button nose and strep throat.
Whilst across this dark street sleeping policemen sleep,
uninterested in career or ambition, permitted an image here and
an image there, a queue on cue.

The beetle wears that look of incomprehension I know so well,
crushed in Saussure's Great-Language-Machine scandal.
Metonymy left and metaphor to my right. Cogs within wheels.

Some say he received a postcard, replied with one, by return.

Fish Cake

Sky = mackerel

+

Earth = herring

Where sunlight cascades broken
Cloud metaphor for front or chemical
Reaction
In the case of memory picks up smells
Cut grass runs into silage
Sledgehammer punches glass
What the front half doesn't
Choice murk greys and browns
Needs a good oily fish
Unidentifiable grey

Woodpecker

Looks like I'll outlive the risk and timber falling
Up here the light knocks against objects flashing and pazzazz
Tap the woodpecker's tap 'Yum, yum' then 'Keep off!'

Martial, Book V Poem 20

If only you and I, dearest Martial,
Could fritter our days endlessly idle,
If we discovered free time, 'The Good Life',
Ignorant of big houses and 'Big Names',
Or the boring laws and their dusty courts—
No, for us: bridle-ways, chatter, the baths,
The Virgin's Aqueduct, bookstalls, the shade
Of urban gardens, drinking in 'The Sights',
The gymnasium—our daily routine.
But the state-of-play is neither's got it,
The good times sinking down as each sun sets.
So every day we loafed, chalked up as debts;
Wouldn't every man live, if he knew how,
Giving it all away to here and now?

Fly By Night

Badly constructed fifties and sixties semis
Street to street bomb-damage up
The hill home, One 11s' signature, noses like zeppelins
We need dates, times, then days wave after wave after cold
Front the bad weather and twin-engined bluebottles'
Crystal mandibles, children's noses flat to the bow-window
Crushed to the same degree of terror, and the same
Chipped smiles of 1940. What made the newspapers.

Board Games

Green Shield Stamps and a chat
The circle square and not a penny
Bread cut flat
But all in the tips
A block of cheddar
Hard as your breast-bone
A cradled paradise
And ten years the trucks passing
Eyes coated with filmy dust
One Monday lunchtime
A conjuror's trick
Tea steeping in three dimensions
Lemons a hazard yellow
I bought you soap from Lush
And Rock's Organic Lemonade

1984

Air in space of a wing and profit for proof do the work obviously
And us hapless apes count the lovely big coins and our stars,
Dirt under nails, a mess of layers, like to unlike for the eight hour stretch.
The point of seeing metaphor, ah, the responsibility,
Responsibilities old and new run freely as the water
To dissolve and change names, reappear all around—
One lone sparrow on the line.
The stars being of human flesh beside my future
Landed on the doormat
The quarter-light projects fields to sky
For which there is no interior philosophy let alone an answer
Next to light gurgles and runs out of the drains.
Stark as that.

Deep Breath

Drink the dark and endless ocean
A man who sold toys on the beach
Counts the buttons and butterfly nuts
Sold tattoos and silhouettes to the government.

Red Dots

Glide about the streets—you couldn't make it up
At least I couldn't, looking for any excuse to glide about—
A soap dispenser, light through the head,
Feet feel like chops, the shirt mint green.
Sunlight outside reflected a downward motion
Of pale leaves. The loss to half an hour's reflection,
Fatal in this context, benign in others, speaks the power of 'not'.

Choo-choo

Little grease spot—as zero as kiss as mouth to oh yes
Where is the author strategically placed, attendant police sirens
                                                    like opera singers?
And this after the introductions, the count in, comprise a novel,
Image sited above immediate proof the impression a pink pinch of sunlight
A glinting silver hatchet ready for its perfection of use.
The cross-section reveals poetry peeled back to the DNA

Converse

Printed in old type
Holly materialises fussing about
The office door, bags of new clothes
Two pairs of Converse one knee up
Bag folded and tucked (must be a shirt in that one) under
Chin to flip the latch free
Up right hand
Bargains galore.

'Good to see you Holly.'

Martial, Book V Poem 34

To you, my parents, Fronto and Flaccilla, I leave
    to your tutelage, my darling sweet girl
Erotion, so she needn't be scared of the dark
    Underworld, or the sharp yelps of Hell's hound.
By six days she fell short of six years this winter,
    cheated of the delights of life to come.
Let her dance and swing between you two great parents,
    repeating my name as her baby-talk.
Let not the grass weigh heavily on her bones, nor
    the earth: she trod not heavily on you.

Least Most

A black Renault Savanna with 'pig fucker' aerosoled down the nearside rear
wing.
Design is more important than Art: Exhibit One. It touches people with
lessons
To be learnt in a world where gambling means saving and Nectar points
Mean prizes and prizes mean.
Or food. Hum the tune as you go along,
Adoring you unconditionally the authentic 'I' of intertextuality.
'Offices' equal offices. Broader term, 'office life'.
As the details speak for themselves I realise orange rhymes with language.

Il Penseroso

I don't want this to turn into a showcase for Michelle and her friends.
Finches peck in a clockwise clockwork movement.
If you want to know, I come here to drink, perhaps helps me start early.
On the corner Michelle re-materialises heavy as a fly, uncharmed by your
charms —
The speckled wave: metaphor for our two voices the eyes pecked out
But the notes survive a lukewarm twelve minutes in outline of the shrieks.
The very next day clouds float above power cables
For now a sparkled wave stands in too —
Dissolves me into many ecstasies, which leads one to ask
Where's the coincidence, in what endless seamlessness?

Rather Like Orchestration

A future becomes a present conjured from a diary.
People walking over the silver bridge.
Nobody goes to sleep these days because no one is allowed,
The top light remains on, the one in the hallway
Projects a strange orange shaft that myths are spun from
Maybe God lives there, rubbing shoulders with Venus
And other candidates for the top job.
That's my view from the stairwell 70 or 80 feet up:
That reading brings no rest, that buttons shine straight,
While easterlies rub windows and trees shiver,
Want to come inside, huddle close by the fire we don't have?
You make it up as you go along, because you know you can
Provide alternatives, people amongst their own thoughts,
Their own egos and silver rain flutters to a predestined destination.
Well, that is if you believe in God (any god). I do not.

The Americans talk like robots at the corner table
Conducting war,
It's some party.
And that makes communication a problematic unravelling of history,
And as for my invaded personal space—*that* dark night of the soul—
The treadmill to the stars is where I'm stuck,
Chilly, chilly enough to bang gloved hands together, boom, boom.

These ruminations the thumbnails of self-regard
Block out all the lights.
Yesterday evening was an eclipse,
The moon high in our smoky latitude,
Those almost imperceptible indentations, ghosts
Of a physical presence sweep around to plant the scissor kick.

Oyster Card

'Cummin' Up!' is the eatery of choice on the A2, the one for me.
I see the world from that porthole, scoffing chicken wings, chips, a Coke.
The buses are regular, pillar-box red, and the drivers happy,
Sometimes not. It's all a bit of a lottery that business,
Where you can't predict outcomes.
Never was that good managing the guesswork.

There are distances travelled though the gaps
Between tyres and curb remain fairly constant.
Journeys, trips: a dirty white container truck
(foreign plates), neatly behind a bendy bus
Whisking an OAP 250 yards up to the fork.

Her GP supplies comfort and pharmaceuticals.
She was wearing a navy coat, Burberry shopping bag,
Can't remember the rest, but the artic is probably
Central European, Czech, Hungarian. Polish even.
Heading our way up the Roman road to the Midlands, up west.

Designs

Every evening the light lowers

To a green effect of Venetian blinds

Reflecting broad daylight

Up the blue-grey wall.

An illusion the ventriloquist

Muttered aloud—who's there—

More a squawk of disagreement

Where the statement

Obviously shapes the choice

Of floral patterning thirty years'

Ago, my mother's itinerary

Ordered from the catalogue

'24th August 1976'

Mixed media—pencil, scribbled on card

Action before utterance

Utterance before thought

Caption before action

Clap the draw shut.

Full of must.

Martial, Book V Poem 37

A girl whose singing was sweeter than a swan's song,
Gentle as a lamb of Phalantine Galaesus,
As precious as the shellfish reared from Lucrine beds,
Who you'd not replace with Erythrean pearls,
Or freshly culled tusks of Indian elephants,
Or a crisp new fall of snow as white as lilies,
Whose hair blonde as fleeces of the Baetic flocks,
Or Rhineland braids, or golden as a pet dormouse,
Whose breath was sweet as beds of Paestan roses,
Or this summer's honey dripping from Attic combs,
Or a ball of amber full of life snatched away;
In comparison the peacock's a dowdy bird,
The squirrel vermin, and the phoenix deadly dull.
Erotion's ashes alive on a warm pyre,
Who harsh Fate ruled her torn from me, a life cut short
Of its sixth winter, and one hardly begun,
All my love, all my joy, my playground friend, all gone.
But my dear Paetus insists I cease my weeping,
Beating his chest, pulls out his own hair by the roots,
'You should be ashamed, blubbing for a wretched slave,
I had to bury my wife, but I carry on,
She was popular, and a woman from good stock.'
Who possesses more fortitude than our Paetus?
Endowed with her twenty million he goes on!

Moment

When this, the present is all crossed out.

Michelle jiving

'We were made for each other,' you said

And left, slamming the door hinges jolted

Door swinging opens

My life forever

About the Mountain

Up here the farmers drive Toyotas and school the sheep like
    arguments.

Sons ride mountain bikes hurled through no network
Up the leeward slope, Space and Time sparkling yellow
Spanking new as a recent shower.

The top's a place for conversation.

When behind the next peak the next thought stacked with the rest
    to a beacon point
In line a pair of buzzards fetch round the bell-shaped summit.

Views to the Irish Sea and its breakers.

And after reading aloud John James' 'The Conversation'
I was saving up for a rainy day over the clouds, you noted

'That apple was very nice,' at 637 metres floating above
    Uwich-mynydd

This twenty-eighth day of September two thousand
And six, the way food can only taste that good

After a three hundred meter ascent traversing the thistle path—

The plastic carrier bag we carried snacks in
(Your apple included, as the batteries were
Not with the rubber torch) ripples like flame

—above harum-scarum slopes, below helter-skelter scree—

Then out of earshot carried off with the booming winds and the
    signal gone

Honeymoon

The bath you arise from clean as a goddess.

Swathed in white and a big smile to boot

Crowned turban-like, towels wrapped about

You flappy corner tucked in

At the armpit worn like a mini-dress

The bruised and blistered toe

Descent from the mountain zigzagging up

The argument signed off all discussion under black

Clouds, all the sing-song hills zipping along

Commands and questions, 'sing if you're glad

To be gay, sing if you're happy this way . . . '

And the deep 'V' of your cunt below . . . .

First tea, then a mug full of chocolatey coffee.

History of the Good

We all believe in doing good

Making goods is the one true good

The highest good at the lowest cost

Making a second party sell your goods to a third is the ultimate good

As time passes by, progress is to the good, in a new disguise history floats away to the Twentieth Century signature, the infinite high note of the penny whistle

A 'c' true and clear

The Auburn Stunner
(after Apollinaire)

I'm standing here in front of you all a man of sound mind
Knowing life and of death equal to what any other citizen might know
Enduring the ups and downs of love
Persuading others occasionally of his ideas
Knowing a multitude of tongues
Travelling far and wide
Who saw the war in the Artillery and the Infantry
Fragment through the skull trepanned under chloroform
Losing all his good comrades in the unspeakable bloodbath
I know the old and the new as only a lonely man is able to know
So let's not fuss today over this war
Between us and between our mates
I'll be the judge of this interminable argument the formal versus
    the free-form Order V Adventure

Your mouth fashioned in the mirror of the one true God's
Mouth which is the one order
Be gentle as you measure us
Against the fops of perfect orderliness
We live life as variously as possible

We are not your adversaries
We want to offer you huge and foreign lands
Where the exotic flower gives itself to those who want to pick it
In that place there are new sparks of colours never seen
A thousand indeterminate ghosts
Who insist on reality
We want to explore goodness the bountiful enormous country of peace
Then there's Time one can ignore or embrace
Pity us who tirelessly resist at the borders
Of endlessness and of that to come
Pity us for our errors pity us for our wrongs

Here strides the mid-summer season of violence
And my innocence is dead where the Spring is late

O sun this is the time of the burning of Reason
    And I'm waiting
So I will inevitably track the aristocratic and comely profile
Which she traces to entice me to love her alone
She floats nearby and reels me in as filings in magnetic fields
    She has that ruby charm
    Totally gorgeous coppery fuzz

Her hair blazes golden
A long-lasting light burst
Or flares in slow motion
As the tea-roses are lost

But laugh laugh at me
You men all over this nation but particularly all you locals
There are countless tales I dare not share
Countless tales you won't allow me to share
Pity me

Goering

What is little known (but true): Hermann Goering was
    Millwall's Number One fan.

At the Den, the main stand was destroyed by sustained bomb-
    damage in '43.

That must have quite put the Reichmarschall's nose out of
    joint. The moral?

Fewer visits to the Wolfsschanze, and more time 'with your
    family' at Carinhall,

This is where little narratives, short stories, telling tales in the
    Black Forest gets you.

Lost, disoriented, without a map, compass, direction, or mind.
    Look! Look!

Here's a trail of breadcrumbs to eat (you won't starve) leading
    out of the dark wood

To a clearing and a gingerbread house, ablaze with
    houselights.

Guess what? Hansel and Gretel are safe and home,

Baked bread and cookies, fresh and warm!

Open Browser

Those that shuffle out at Chelsfield complete
The daily round of their day, sun up sun
Down, exhaustion a bonus to the pay
(salaried not waged)—listen, look in-
To your electronic device the last
Human contact on earth, then they're
Gone to another place and so are we:

Keep it plain, keep it simple, plan the note
To yourself, the information life's
Secret, how one might proceed, go on and
Impress management, where the lives of others
Lead (a handbook is what we need or text-
Book) you lose track, forget your place;
Jot it down on a Post-It, reminder
Of the here and now slips away where then
As now you're off the rails it's too
Late to use the experience, the learning
Curve too tight a curve to fit the present
Data of various circumstances—
The pressure to know what you mean and meant:

Love the matter and difficulty re-
Turns to the stranger easier to love
With the gaze to engage at a bite point,
Tags, casual browsing; data teems, tips
Those projected against the mesh of lives . . .
The memory revisits me, the truth
And pleasure, one and twin, the train journey
No one-way looking, no one way looking-
Glass, an eye on the site now, then then, then
One in many, love multiplies those that
Listen, watch, reply . . . wireless connections,
Invisible stretch, ties home those that come to
Those that rise through ten thousand laptops.

Tryst

We were due to meet at 11, but I had you pencilled for 11.30. You didn't turn up, and I don't believe I let you down. Still, no-one will ever guess the scale of my error.

By 11.45 the door firmly in its jamb, a folded square of blue notepaper wedged, and the key flipped easily in its lock, I was gone, phuff!

Self-Portrait in a Bathroom Mirror

I'm sitting here in 1970, Christopher Middleton

And John Ashbery are 44 (or 43), Frank O'Hara

Dead four years—today's lesson:

'How syllables work' IM-PORT-

ANT, important for me (having wiped

Round the tidemark with an old sponge,

Like a good boy, whoops! My dad's

Face flannel!), and the individual

Using the peach-coloured bath next,

(Daddy Muck Bath, we'll call him)

'IMPORTANT: Do Not Use

Abrasives When Cleaning'

The notice I read out to the world

Mouthing each sound, first

Of the fibreglass baths I sensed I was

Comfortable in and informed about,

A reassuring warmth about it impossible

But important to describe

Impossible but important:

A meandering odyssey stopping off

To take in the sights and the poetry

And prose of Christopher

Middleton and John Ashbery,

Like Greek islands.

Love for Frank

O'Hara's 'I do this, I do that'

A second stop

Echoed here and echoes here.

Martial, Book X Poem 47

Which ingredients will fulfil a full life,
Most loved and cherished friend, Martial? These are they:
A family endowment, money not earned;
Estates managed well; a constantly stoked fire;
Never practise law, hardly don a toga;
Of sound mind and body, slim, lean and fit;
Tactful and candid, grooming friends of like mind;
Vivacious dinner guests with simple cuisine;
Evenings without a drink, relaxed, worry-free;
A nuptial bed not prudish, but decent;
A deep sleep to quicken the dark night's passing;
Believe in yourself and expect little more;
Neither side-step your end, nor dash towards it.

Puerile Allegations

Puerile. From puer.

Check the email for a few points

Time to eat, thankfully

My budget runs the costs lower

My bucket of stars where every tooth

Falls into place alongside every other

Perfect molar, incisor, or canine.

Twenty-four at the last count

As many as the hours a day holds,

With the advent of middle age

Retention of the aforesaid set

Moves up the 'to do' list,

Now a priority

Teeth, hours—the mnemonics

Solid as the wobbly molar

Lower right, assigned A5

Questions of Beauty

Where is Keats when I need him?

What level of discourse do you expect from tee-shirts?

Parole et langue, a place to drop *stuff* off,

His and hers, but which one is which,

Which one is? Bags, photographs,

Personalised matching towels!

Monogrammed handkerchiefs!

Sunny days (mostly real) genuine

Angels in the angles down the path

Passed the tree under which he wrote

That poem after bumping into, STC,

Literally—to the front garden gate and fireflies

Alight then a faded yellow . . .

Where *is* he, I need answers—

Circumstances are pressing, time running out

The air from a tired puncture or pressure valve,

We all wear Converse now life is

That which the waves draw back

Supposedly to the soft edges

Under this not so new government,

That vase of his: is beauty such a cold thing,

Knocked carelessly from the mantelpiece?

The inundation didn't halt at Dover

Beach, it never did and it never will

Parole ou langue, in the Uniform Edition?

Two Times Table

I am starting another piece of 'creative writing' to twin with my slice of homemade cake. Chocolate coloured it doesn't taste of chocolate, but it does of cake. I must return to this piece of 'creative writing'. It decays like an isotope, with all the decency of a hat. Under the hat alternatives to shout out might be, 'Glasses with a funny nose! A moustache!' A new identity credible enough to fool the bull terrier at the cast iron gate of the house opposite. House of my dreams.

The English Peacemaker

A lunch-time bet both ways, presenting myself
At the booth, slip and notes in hand to pay up,

I'd turned over the conundrum, testing the mileage:
What Americans measure in hours the English

Stretch furlong by furlong of countryside,
Thoroughbreds neck and neck not a fag paper

Between—there's probably more truth than speculation
Attached to the steeplechase than to me frozen as the gun

Barrel of presence swivels towards my chest
Like a standard service Webley Mk 1 revolver,

The orientation of cartridge to chamber left me
Mayakovsky's dilemma with a pastoral twist

At the first report to the favourite's temple.

Hurdy Gurdy Man

Scene: a university town, middle-England satellite council estates
Flags hang between shop-fronts with the faces of peasants to shoot at,
Compose a quiet spectacle and Michelle's cousin Bob as was
To be predicted, down and out, selling the *Big Issue* at the shopping centre.

In the plate-glass, kitchen and bathroom fittings, chill of the gilt,
Chromium and formica, but do you know what's funny, really
Hilarious (it's vitreous humour)—'Reflections on a Plastic Bath'—

His new work of Romantic Imagination, breath hot on the glass

A sandwich down in two bites, gorge rising with the third,
The kiosk supplied more comfortable data of the glossy leaflet variety,
More a lifetime in quiet curries than the expensive Cornish-china-clay
    treatment
Afforded monographs, cataloguing country estates: a life left in lots

Posterior to posterity . . . . Bob's bottle of Stella frothing like squash,
Information gathered to the hip, salsa-like,
A corn doll you can't tell the sex of

—'Nicole Kidman's double' and 'do-able'—(I need a shower)

Alongside hedge funds which flew into his mouth
The attractive man with the unattractive laugh
The flutter flies about the lips resembles dead flies
My imagination (I know what you mean?), have a knack for,

The shapeless package gaffered to the dash will tear
Your head clean off, oozing yellow ooze and nails—
The *T.V. Guide* and the perfect aesthetic of delivery in a human
Bomb the natural complement to a 'Christmas Special,' charades,

'An Evening with Alfred Brendel' or consequences,
And a Christmas tree no one comes home to . . .

Saskia, do you remember *that* fiery reindeer?
Window open, sash broken

                                    a single light bulb sails through

The wild air, shafts of energy
Generate a little beam next door above

The naked bodies, the shocking whitenesses,
A male's back against Michelle's tanned thigh
Drawn towards the dim screen swallowed the white
Dot the whole globe with us pinned quivering to a full-stop

Now in paper and bound within boards the plot.
A steal, pasted to my c.v., a price tag to boot.

First Idea

Sheets straight from the line smelt sharp as winter, stiff and permeated with frost, are laid out on the tiled floor, a vast white picnic.

Objects of Desire

Sipping tea from a Claes Oldenburg mug
The instinct to go on naming
And gaze with the broken line—
Lists of outlets to match.

He beams at me, one of the kids
Doing colouring-in,
Pushes on through the instant,
Moon greasy as a beach ball,

Tomatoes fat as boxing gloves—
Photos of boxing gloves fattening tomatoes.

Forward of this point in the luminous
Static air, these days whisk past
As I attempt cheer, and the chocolate fudge
Sundaes have taken over the palace.

Text

Derrida, Foucault, Barthes, Lacan,

Saussure, lined up in this circle

Paterson, Farley, Armitage, Padel

Form a line opposite

The penguins waddle across

'No texting aloud,' the sign says.

A tale to share over dinner,

Once upon a time, the text

Was unhappy, boo-hoo, boo-hoo

'The slippage of the signifier

Across the signifier makes

The signifier the signified

For another signifier.'

But The Modern Poets left no message

At the beep, just static, flat-lining

To Alpha Centauri _____.

Meanwhile on the ground

Les Tricoteuses knit one pearl one knit one,

'Di Dum, Di Dum, Di Dum, Di Dum, Di Dum'

How They Brought the Good News from Ghent to Aix

At the kitchen window cats' heads float like balloons.
R.B.'s voice whirrs and squeaks through a wax cylinder, via the
    World Wide Web,
And Labour are expecting a bruising night,
Some policy decisions snatched from damp air.
Snarling traffic queues along the A2.

Sediments whirl around the bottom of the washing-up bowl
Or sink, nothing clean,
Nothing sweet this 3rd May 2007.

You wash, I'll dry. Surrey and Kent kiss at the garden wall.

By morning the World reborn fresh and new.
But who sat in my garden c.1890,
The *Middlemarch* moral experiment in full-swing,
With Robert Browning dead and gone?

Martial, Book X poem 61

Too soon a walking shadow, 'Erotion lies here',
    criminally cheated of her sixth year.
Whoever you are who buys my garden and house,
    offer up a gift to her little ghost:
Your household's safe, will remain your home through the years,
    this headstone your one grief and cause for tears.

A Table

Out of the woods and into history. Talk above, discourse below the oak. Table legs thick as a maid's, no one day without a conversation above beeswax polish above a shine.

There once was an oak tree and it told stories. One of those stories is this table, and lives were framed. My grandfather was a fireman on a steam locomotive, which disappeared into a tunnel. On the other side of the hill he was a train-driver, 'choo, choo'. He smoked like a train, then he died. This made my mother sad. I didn't know mummies cried. Now all the mummies cry.

My grandmother wore a floral apron. While my grandfather stoked his train, she fed the iron-black coal-fired range. On Mondays she washed all day, and so hard all the furniture popped out into the garden.

The table occupies the same space, reflects the same light it occupied and reflected circa 1920 when it was made, not by craftsmen, but by a machine process to look like it was hand-built.

The table I'm writing on is like a microphone. I'm reeling this off from the knots and grain of amber wood.

Genuine oak, fake skills.

The table proves the passing of time, and paradoxically, the synchronicity of time. I've just bruised my left hip, challenging the theory, knocking into its bevelled top, as I slid on to the upright dining chair, one of four that match, and start a lunch of baked beans on toast I'd purchased earlier this morning from the supermarket. Now the meal is spilt, lunch not quite begun and not quite finished.

Lightning Source UK Ltd.
Milton Keynes UK
24 August 2010

9 781844 714902